IT'S A WONDERFUL WORLD

Jess French

DK Penguin Random House

Author Jess French
Illustrator Aleesha Nandhra

Consultant Louise Mair
Editors Sophie Parkes, Sarah MacLeod
Project Art Editor Charlotte Bull
Designed by Sadie Thomas
Managing Editor Penny Smith
Senior Production Editor Nikoleta Parasaki
Production Controller John Casey
Jacket Coordinator Issy Walsh
Deputy Art Director Mabel Chan
Publisher Sarah Larter

First published in Great Britain in 2022 by
Dorling Kindersley Limited
DK, One Embassy Gardens, 8 Viaduct Gardens,
London, SW11 7BW

The authorised representative in the EEA is
Dorling Kindersley Verlag GmbH. Arnulfstr. 124,
80636 Munich, Germany

Copyright © 2022 Dorling Kindersley Limited
A Penguin Random House Company
10 9 8 7 6 5 4 3 2 1
001–326523–Mar/2022

A CIP catalogue record for this book
is available from the British Library.
ISBN: 978-0-2415-3354-3

Printed and bound in China

For the curious
www.dk.com

MIX
Paper from
responsible sources
FSC™ C018179

This book was made with Forest Stewardship
Council™ certified paper – one small step in
DK's commitment to a sustainable future.

For more information go to
www.dk.com/our-green-pledge

contents

introduction

Our planet is enormous, isn't it? Have you ever looked out at a vast ocean or a huge mountain and wondered what your place in the world is? I have. It is easy to feel small and insignificant in those places, especially when the Earth seems so giant. But even though you are just one person, you have the power to make incredible changes. Changes that will alter the future for the animals, plants, and people that live on our wonderful planet. And our planet needs people like you more than ever – people that will make the right choices and help it to recover.

We humans haven't always been very kind to our home. As a species, we have made a lot of mistakes, and many animals and plants have suffered as a result. But the world is still full of wonder. It is still full of incredible habitats, fascinating animals, and extraordinary plants. Our world is weird, wonderful, and sometimes downright gross. But most importantly, our perfect planet can look after itself if we just stop causing it harm. It's not much to ask really, is it?

So come with me on a journey around our wonderful world, and together let's learn how we can protect it.

Jess French

Jess French

where are we?

Our planet, Earth, is just one tiny piece of the giant jigsaw we call the Universe. For humans and other animals, Earth is a very special place, because it's the only planet we know of that supports life.

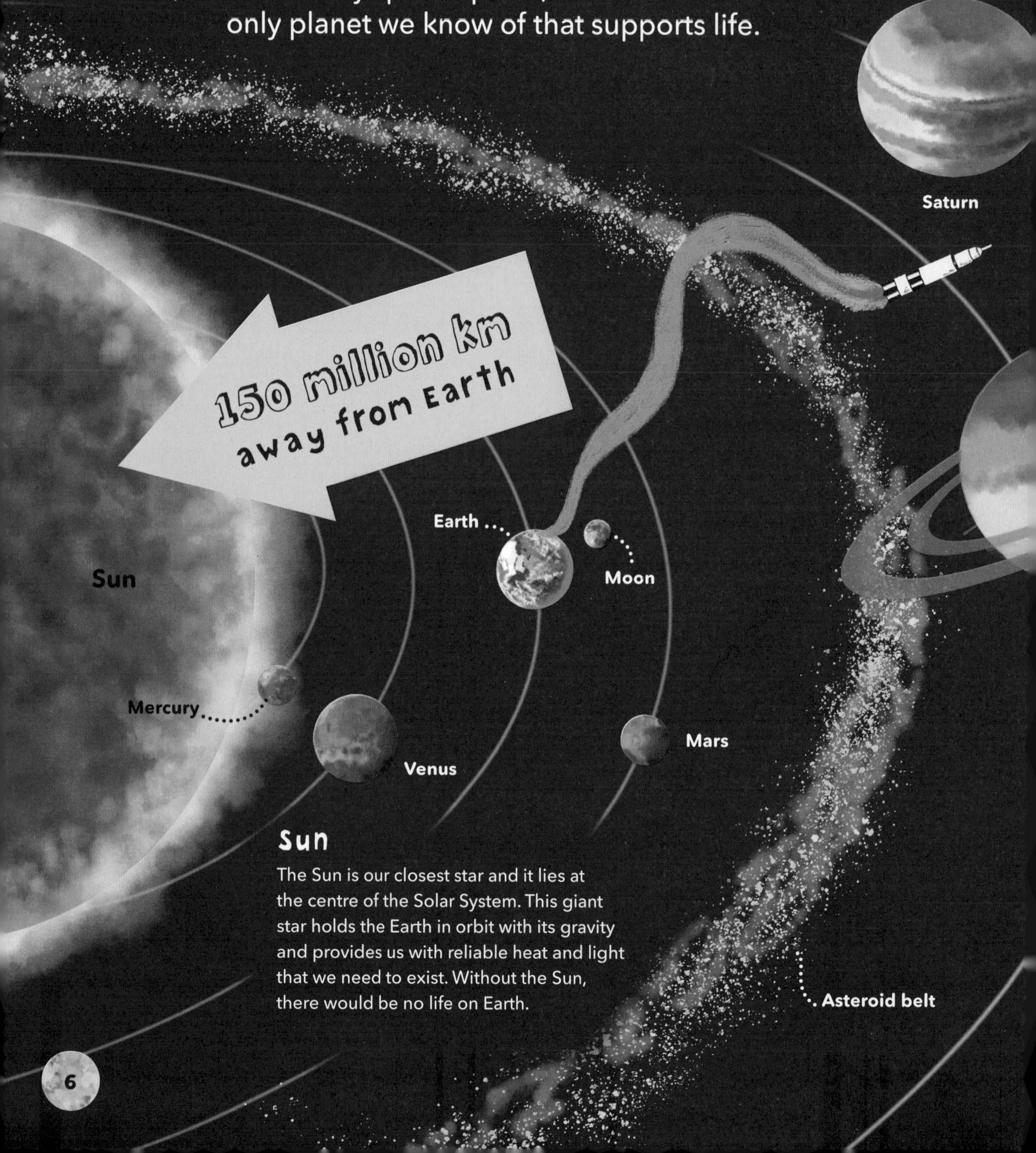

Saturn

150 million km away from Earth

Sun

Earth

Moon

Mercury

Venus

Mars

Sun

The Sun is our closest star and it lies at the centre of the Solar System. This giant star holds the Earth in orbit with its gravity and provides us with reliable heat and light that we need to exist. Without the Sun, there would be no life on Earth.

Asteroid belt

Comet

Uranus

Neptune

Earth's future

Lots has changed on Earth in the billions of years since life began here, but from space it has looked more or less the same. Years from now, it will probably still look like a small blue dot, but much will have changed. The decisions we make today will shape those changes, so it's up to us to make the right choices.

The Sun and all the objects that orbit it are collectively called the Solar System. The Solar System is found in a spiral-shaped galaxy called the Milky Way.

Jupiter

Earth

Water, oxygen, and warmth are crucial for life to exist. Earth is enveloped by a layer of gases called the atmosphere, which keeps us warm and provides us with oxygen to breathe. Water is also in plentiful supply - it covers more than 70 per cent of Earth's surface.

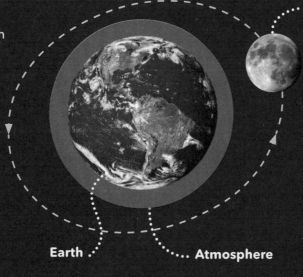

Moon

Moon

The Moon orbits Earth. It is not as vital to life on our planet as the Sun, but it does have a big impact. The Moon's gravity controls our tides, and some animals even use the Moon to navigate.

Earth

Atmosphere

Atmosphere

Our planet, like many others, is surrounded by a blanket of gases called the atmosphere. When the right amount of gases are in the atmosphere, the planet is kept at the perfect temperature to sustain life. Our atmosphere is split into five major layers.

700 to 10,000 km
(440 to 6,200 miles)

80 to 700 km
(50 to 440 miles)

50 to 80 km
(31 to 50 miles)

12 to 50 km
(7.5 to 31 miles)

0 to 12 km
(0 to 7.5 miles)

Meteor

Ozone layer
The ozone layer is Earth's sunscreen – it protects our planet from the Sun's most damaging rays.

Some of the Sun's heat bounces off Earth's surface and out through the atmosphere, while some gets trapped inside.

The denser the atmosphere, the more heat is trapped.

Greenhouse effect

When there are extra gases in the atmosphere, it gets denser and traps more heat, so Earth gets hotter. This is called the greenhouse effect.

Aeroplane

Hot air balloon

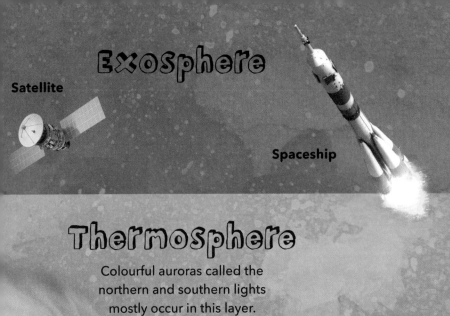

Exosphere

Satellite

Spaceship

Thermosphere

Colourful auroras called the northern and southern lights mostly occur in this layer.

Aurora

Mesosphere

Stratosphere

The ozone layer is found here. Unlike in the troposphere, where it gets cooler as you move higher, temperatures in the stratosphere increase the higher you go.

Weather balloon

Troposphere

This is the layer we live in.

climate change

Human behaviour has harmed Earth's natural greenhouse. Over the last 100 years, we have burned fossil fuels, cleared forest, and created waste on an enormous scale. All of these activities release greenhouse gases that cause the planet to heat up. To prevent temperatures rising even more, we must change our ways.

Global warming is melting Earth's precious polar ice. This leads to more global warming, rising sea levels, and extreme weather.

cutting greenhouse gases

There are many simple changes we can all make to reduce the amount of greenhouse gases we produce. Try walking instead of taking a car, using energy-saving lightbulbs that you switch off when you leave a room, and taking shorter showers.

Wind and solar energy are renewable sources that are better for the planet.

Water

Water is extremely precious, because all animals rely on it to survive. Without water, life on Earth would simply not be possible. The amount of water on Earth never changes – instead it is recycled, moving from place to place, powered by energy from the Sun.

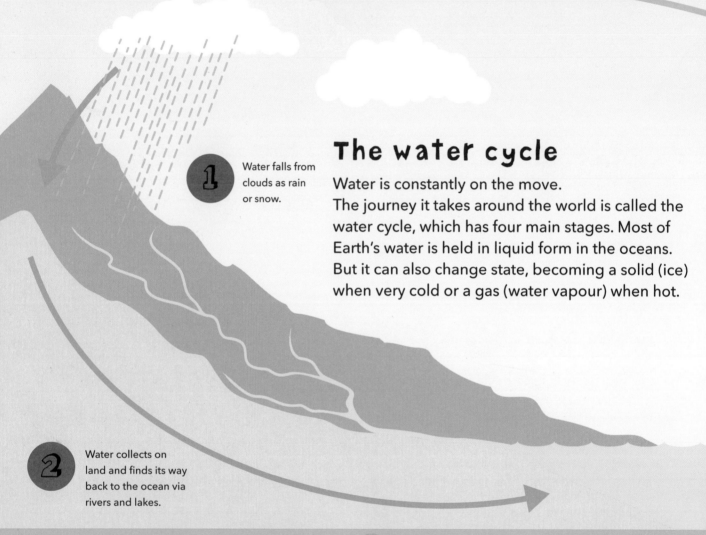

1 Water falls from clouds as rain or snow.

The water cycle

Water is constantly on the move. The journey it takes around the world is called the water cycle, which has four main stages. Most of Earth's water is held in liquid form in the oceans. But it can also change state, becoming a solid (ice) when very cold or a gas (water vapour) when hot.

2 Water collects on land and finds its way back to the ocean via rivers and lakes.

How can you save water?

Turn off the tap while you brush your teeth to save water.

Save up bathwater to water your plants and flush your toilet.

Instead of baths, take short showers, which use less water.

Use a water butt to collect rainwater for watering the garden.

Water and people

Sadly, not everyone has access to clean water or a private toilet. Around the world, more than 2 billion people have no choice but to drink polluted water. In some places, people have to walk many hours to collect clean water. Polluted water can cause diseases such as cholera, typhoid, and dysentery, which can be fatal.

4 As it rises, the water cools and condenses to form clouds.

3 Water warmed by the Sun becomes water vapour and rises (evaporates).

Less than 1% of Earth's water is available for drinking.

Save water from boiling vegetables and pasta to water houseplants.

Run the dishwasher and washing machine on short, cold cycles.

Get dripping taps fixed quickly to avoid wasting water.

Water pollution

Water can be polluted in many ways:

Leaks and spills from oil pipelines

Litter from the land

Illegal dumping of waste and chemicals from factories

Flushing inappropriate things down the toilet

Run off of fertilizers from agriculture

Nature in balance

As humans living on Earth, we are part of a phenomenal natural system. Our planet is brilliant at regulating itself and when humans don't interfere, life exists in a perfect balance. Unfortunately, human actions do mess with these natural systems and if we do not change soon, we may tip the scales totally out of balance.

Burning fossil fuels releases large amounts of carbon dioxide and other dangerous gases into the atmosphere.

Ocean
Oceans take in carbon dioxide. They also absorb heat and spread it around the planet.

Nature's balance in action

Next time you are in a forest, look up at the canopy. You will notice that the trees don't touch – they grow only as far as the space allows. This is called crown shyness. For the Earth to stay balanced, every living thing must use its fair share of resources, instead of invading the spaces of the things around them.

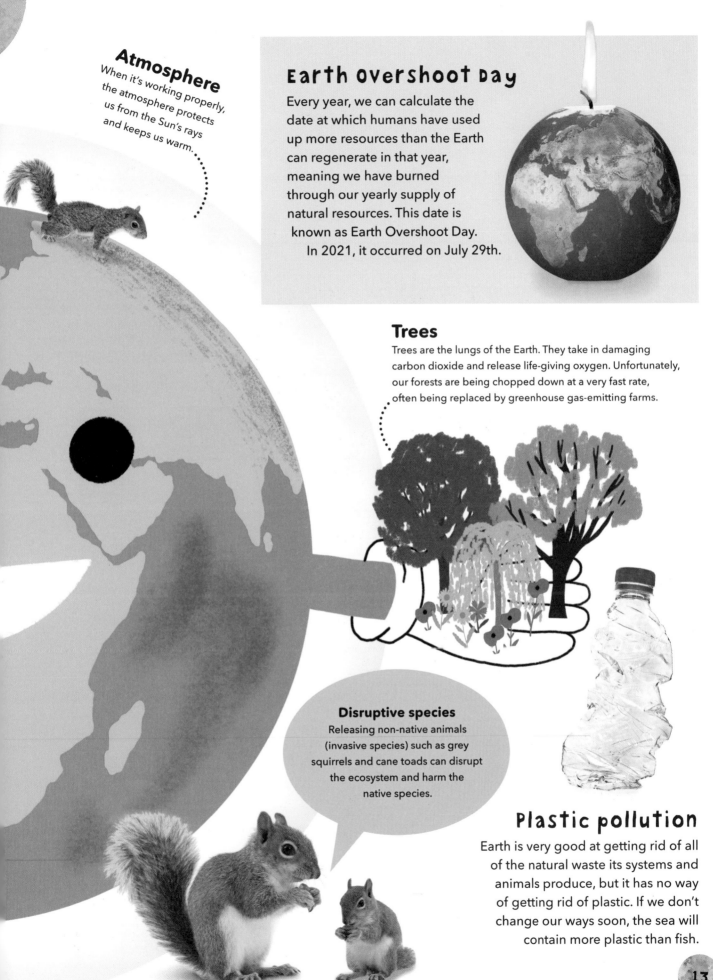

Atmosphere

When it's working properly, the atmosphere protects us from the Sun's rays and keeps us warm.

Earth Overshoot Day

Every year, we can calculate the date at which humans have used up more resources than the Earth can regenerate in that year, meaning we have burned through our yearly supply of natural resources. This date is known as Earth Overshoot Day. In 2021, it occurred on July 29th.

Trees

Trees are the lungs of the Earth. They take in damaging carbon dioxide and release life-giving oxygen. Unfortunately, our forests are being chopped down at a very fast rate, often being replaced by greenhouse gas-emitting farms.

Disruptive species

Releasing non-native animals (invasive species) such as grey squirrels and cane toads can disrupt the ecosystem and harm the native species.

Plastic pollution

Earth is very good at getting rid of all of the natural waste its systems and animals produce, but it has no way of getting rid of plastic. If we don't change our ways soon, the sea will contain more plastic than fish.

Plants

Plants are responsible for maintaining our climate, stabilizing the ground beneath our feet, and filtering the air we breathe. Spending time in green spaces can make us feel happier and healthier, as plants have been proven to improve our mood.

Oxygen

Carbon dioxide

Photosynthesis

Plants use energy from the Sun to convert water and carbon dioxide into glucose and oxygen. This process is called photosynthesis. By removing carbon dioxide from the atmosphere and storing carbon in their leaves and stems, plants help to combat climate change.

Dragon tree
This tree survives extreme heat by using its long leaves to collect moisture from the air.

Bee orchid

Orchid mantis

Pine trees

Ferns

Flowering plants

There are around 370,000 different types of flowering plant, each with its own unique flower. Some insects have evolved to look like flowers, such as the orchid mantis, which uses its disguise to avoid being spotted by its prey.

Non-flowering plants

The earliest plants did not produce flowers. Many examples of non-flowering plants are still around today, including mosses, ferns, and conifers. Some reproduce by making seeds, while others release spores, which grow into new plants.

Rain cover
Trees can reduce and prevent flooding, as their leaves, branches, and trunks slow the flow of heavy rain on its way to the ground.

Animal homes
Lots of animals, such as this orangutan, make their homes among trees, hedgerows, and other plants.

Fallen leaves
After leaves have fallen to the ground, they get broken down. This feeds the soil and helps new plants to grow.

Holding it together
Roots stabilize soil by holding it in place. Without roots, soil is more easily eroded and landslides are more likely to occur.

Animals that eat only plants are called herbivores. Some animals, such as pandas and koalas, rely on just one species of plant for all of their energy.

Carnivorous plants
In areas with poor-quality soil, it can be tricky for plants to get the nutrients they need. Carnivorous plants, such as pitcher plants, venus fly traps, and sundews, make up for this by eating animals.

The bad
Around two in five plants are in danger of going extinct, thanks to some of the following reasons:

Trees are removed to graze livestock, build human settlements, and grow crops.

The ground is concreted over, making it very difficult for new plants to grow.

The good
We can help plants by buying our food from places that treat plants with respect.

Choose fruit and vegetables that have been sustainably grown and picked locally.

You could even try growing your own fruit and vegetables.

15

Grasses

Grasses are found all over the planet. They are very adaptable and spread easily to new areas, where they stabilize and protect the soil. There are many types of grasslands, from salt marshes and grazing pastures to savannahs and bamboo forests.

Great grasslands

Areas where there isn't enough rain for many trees to grow are covered in grasses. These places support species that graze on the grasses, and predators that stalk the grazers. Savannahs are grasslands found in dry, warm areas. Some African savannahs contain wildlife such as lions, elephants, and zebra.

⚠ The bad

Our grasslands are under threat. This is mainly from humans turning grassland into areas for agriculture, and also grazing too many animals there.

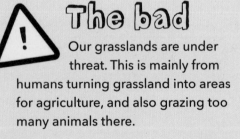

Many butterflies depend on flowers to eat. But many grasslands where flowers grow have become used for agriculture, making it hard for the butterflies to find food.

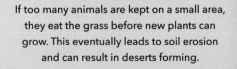

If too many animals are kept on a small area, they eat the grass before new plants can grow. This eventually leads to soil erosion and can result in deserts forming.

Bamboo forest

Although its thick stems and great height makes it look rather tree-like, bamboo is actually a grass! It is the fastest-growing plant on Earth, with some varieties growing almost a metre in a single day. It lives in dense forests where light can't reach the ground, so it grows fast to reach sunlight as quickly as possible.

Grasses are incredibly useful. Humans have found many ways to use them in their day-to-day lives.

How do we use grasses?

We grow cereal crops, which are fed to humans and livestock. These include wheat, rice, and oats.

We build some of our houses and roofs out of bamboo and thatched straw (dried grasses).

The good

Luckily, by changing some of your habits and questioning your choices, you can help grass to thrive.

Stop mowing your lawn so often, and instead let the grass and wildflowers grow to provide nectar for hungry animals in your patch.

Animals can be raised in a way that is less damaging for the planet. If you do buy meat, make sure it has been raised in a sustainable way.

Eat less meat. It will mean that fewer animals will need to be grazed on grasslands, giving grasses a chance to recover.

Algae

From tiny, single-celled organisms to vast strings of seaweed, algae come in many shapes and sizes, and can be found all over the planet. They are most commonly seen in lakes, rivers, and oceans, but can also be found in trees, snow, hot springs, and even lava flows.

Algae is amazing

Like plants, algae convert harmful carbon dioxide into oxygen. Algae also play a vital role in the food cycle: they use up nutrients released by decomposers and form the base of the food chain in many water ecosystems.

Kelp forests provide homes for many animals, such as sea otters, sea urchins, octopuses, baby fish, and seals.

Working together

Algae often form partnerships with other organisms.

Algae and fungi can live together to form lichens. This association benefits both species and is called a symbiotic relationship.

Algae provide reef-building corals with energy and oxygen in exchange for nutrients and shelter.

Algae living within hard corals give them their beautiful colours, from pink or violet, to yellow or blue.

Hippos eat lots of grass. This means their poo is packed with nutrients, making it the perfect food for algae.

.... **Giant kelp**
This species of seaweed can grow to more than 30 m (98 ft) in length.

Algal blooms

Algae is important for the planet, but too much of it in the wrong place can be very damaging. Algal blooms can produce toxins, reduce oxygen levels, and kill plants and animals living nearby. They are often caused by fertilizers washing off farmland into water.

Algal blooms occur when too many nutrients get into water, causing algae to grow out of control.

This cold-loving snow algae lies undisturbed when temperatures are too cold, but bursts into life as snow begins to melt. The pinkish colour of the blooms have earned them the name "watermelon snow".

How to help

There is not one simple way to prevent algal blooms, but there are plenty of things we can do to help.

Wild fish

No fertilizer

Fish farms produce vast amounts of poo, which can lead to algal blooms. Try eating sustainably caught wild fish instead.

Farmers can reduce the amount of fertilizers they use and improve the quality of their soil in other ways.

Mosses

One of the first plants to adapt to life on land, mosses have been around for 450 million years. While they're very basic plants, with no flowers or seeds, mosses are incredibly useful: they stabilize soil, collect water, capture carbon, and provide habitats for all sorts of living things.

Sphagnum moss

Rhizoids

Mosses are very absorbent – sphagnum mosses can soak up more than 20 times their weight in water. They can slow down the flow of rain, which helps prevent flooding.

Unlike most other plants, mosses don't have roots. Instead, they are held in place by branching anchors called rhizoids.

Mosses are often one of the first plants to grow on land that has been damaged by fire. They help reduce post-fire flash flooding and hold soil together, preventing it from eroding.

carbon sponge

Like all plants, mosses absorb carbon dioxide and release oxygen. But they don't take up as much space as trees. Covering walls with moss could be a great way to absorb carbon in cities.

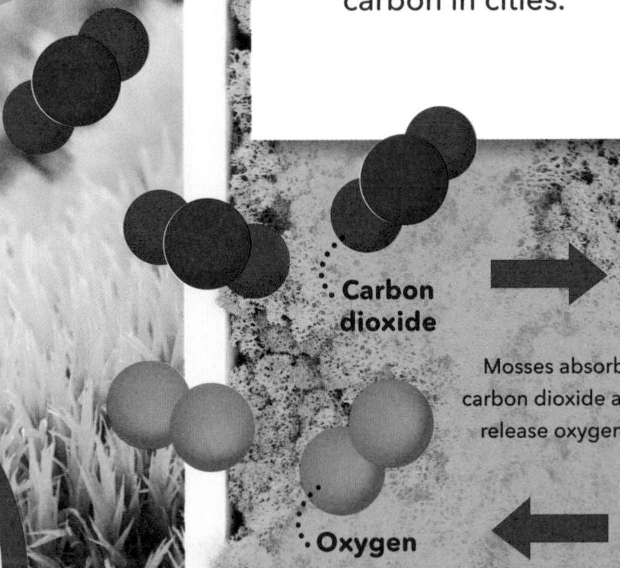

Carbon dioxide

Mosses absorb carbon dioxide and release oxygen.

Oxygen

Birds, squirrels, and other rodents use cosy mosses to line their nests.

Mosses mostly grow in damp environments, but they can survive in many other habitats too, from freezing snowy mountains to baking hot deserts.

Humans have used moss for centuries, whether for stuffing pillows and insulating houses, to putting out fires and dressing wounds.

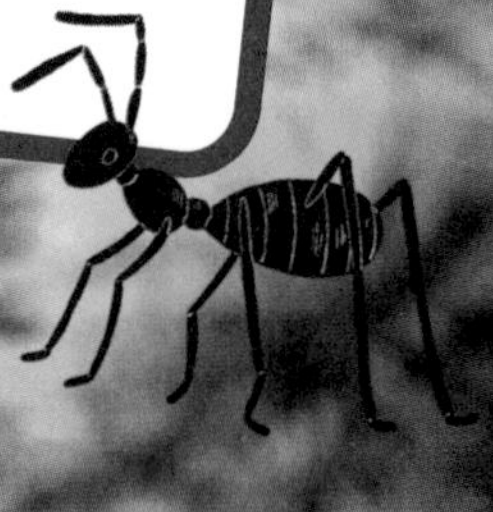

There are more than 10,000 different types of moss.

Fungi

From toadstools that grow in the forest to mould that grows on old bread, fungi come in many shapes and sizes. They are neither animals nor plants and are much larger than the fruiting bodies we see, usually stretching far and wide beneath the surface.

Sometimes a fungus teams up with a living thing called a cyanobacterium or an alga to form lichen. This composite organism can grow on just about any surface.

Scientists believe that only

5%

of fungi have been discovered. We still have lots to learn about these unusual organisms.

Scientists estimate that there are 2 to 4 million different types of fungi, but it's hard to know for sure.

Oregon honey fungus

In Malheur National Forest in Oregon, USA, scientists have discovered a gigantic fungus called the Oregon honey fungus. Its vast network of underground fibres spreads out for many kilometres and each individual can live for thousands of years.

Around 95 per cent of soil-growing plants have fungi called mycorrhiza growing around their roots, helping them draw more nutrients and water from the soil.

The world's first farmers were insects. Just as humans grow crops for food, ants, termites, and ambrosia beetles tend and harvest fungus crops to feed themselves and their babies.

In order to attract flies and other insects to help them reproduce, the odd-looking stinkhorn fungus imitates the pong of a decomposing body.

Ambrosia beetles

Termites

Leaf-cutter ants

Soil

It might not look like much, but soil is crucial to life on land.
Good soils are often brown, soft, and crumbly, but they can be sandy
(in deserts) or squelchy (in bogs) too. Most plants need soil to grow
and survive, and one quarter of all living things live in soil.

Roots
Roots reach down into soil to
anchor a plant in place. They
also take up water and
nutrients from the soil.

Humus
When pieces of dead plant have
broken down, they form a rich,
dark layer on top of the soil,
called humus. It is rich in
water and nutrients.

Soil is vital to life above its surface...

Soil contains
billions of microscopic
organisms, including
bacteria and fungi.

Fungal friends
Sometimes plant roots team
up with fungal networks, in a
combination called a mycorrhiza.
In exchange for sugars, the fungi
provide the roots with extra water
and nutrition from the soil.

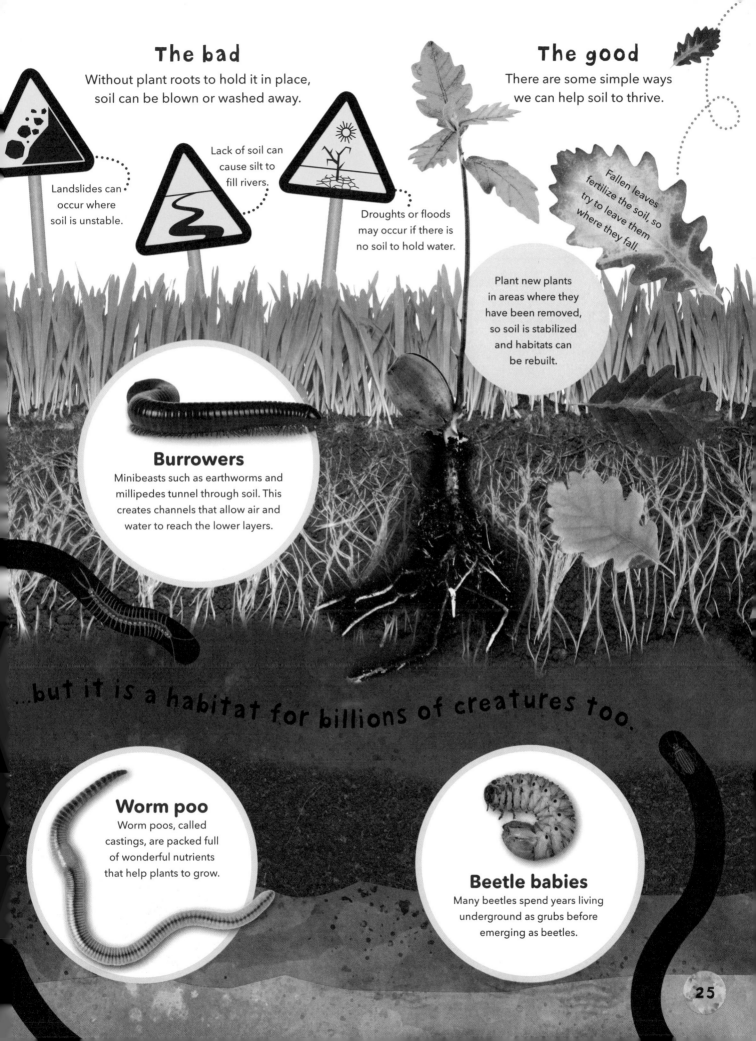

The bad

Without plant roots to hold it in place, soil can be blown or washed away.

Landslides can occur where soil is unstable.

Lack of soil can cause silt to fill rivers.

Droughts or floods may occur if there is no soil to hold water.

The good

There are some simple ways we can help soil to thrive.

Fallen leaves fertilize the soil, so try to leave them where they fall.

Plant new plants in areas where they have been removed, so soil is stabilized and habitats can be rebuilt.

Burrowers

Minibeasts such as earthworms and millipedes tunnel through soil. This creates channels that allow air and water to reach the lower layers.

...but it is a habitat for billions of creatures too.

Worm poo

Worm poos, called castings, are packed full of wonderful nutrients that help plants to grow.

Beetle babies

Many beetles spend years living underground as grubs before emerging as beetles.

Pollination

Around 80% of all flowering plants are pollinated by animals, whether insects, birds, reptiles, or mammals. We often see insects visiting flowers during the day, but many pollinators work hard at night instead.

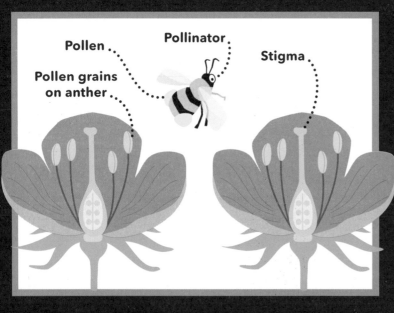

Pollen

Pollinator

Stigma

Pollen grains on anther

what is pollination?

In order for a plant to make seeds, pollen grains must be moved from the male part of one flower (the anther) to the female parts of another (the stigma). Sometimes, pollen can be carried by the wind, but for most flowering plants, it is carried by animals.

Indian carpenter bee
Most bees fly during the day, but a few special species, such as this Indian carpenter bee, work the night shift too.

Only an extremely long proboscis can reach the nectar inside a Madagascar orchid.

The proboscis can reach 23 cm (9 in) long.

Morgan's sphinx moth
This moth has an incredibly long, tube-like mouthpart called a proboscis. This allows it to reach the nectar deep inside tube-shaped flowers that other insects cannot.

Agave
.... flower

Nocturnal animals can be confused by the light of street lamps.

Mexican long-tongued bat

Many species of agave plant rely on Mexican long-tongued bats for pollination and seed dispersal. But in some places, agave crops are being harvested before they can flower and go through pollination.

Masked palm civet

When masked palm civets force their way into Mucuna flowers, they trigger an explosion of pollen. They then carry it to the next flower they visit.

Smelling sweet

Day-blooming flowers often use bright colours to attract pollinators, but without daylight to show off their petals, night-blooming flowers have to use strong scents to attract pollinators instead.

what can we do?

There are a few ways we can help night pollinators do their jobs.

Allow plants to bloom fully before harvesting crops.

Plant night-blooming plants such as honeysuckle and jasmine.

Switch off lights to reduce night-time light pollution.

Moonflower

Night-blooming moonflowers unfurl their petals as the Sun is setting. They release a sweet scent to attract pollinators such as moths and bats.

Seed dispersal

Seeds contain everything that a new plant needs to germinate. However, if they fall directly under their parent plant, they won't have space to grow. Each plant must find a way to send its seeds off to find a new home. This process is called seed dispersal.

Wind
Even a light breeze is enough to lift up the winged seeds of dandelions and carry them away.

Floating seeds
Some seeds float on water and can raft off down rivers. Coconuts have been known to float thousands of kilometres across the ocean before germinating on distant shores.

Tasty fruits
When animals guzzle fruits, they usually swallow the seeds too. The seeds are then carried with the animal until they are pooed out of the other end – in a lovely dollop of fertiliser.

Hold on! Is that poo or a seed?!

Poo pretender

The seeds of *Ceratocaryum argenteum*, a grass-like plant, look and smell like the droppings of an antelope called a bontebok. Dung beetles think they are balls of poo and so roll them off and bury them.

Violent ejection

When sandbox tree seeds are mature, they explode with a loud bang and blast their seeds at about 240 kph (150 mph).

Fur travel

Some seeds have little hooks so they can cling to the fur of passing animals. They get carried to new places to germinate.

Food bodies

Some seeds contain food bodies - tasty bits that make animals want to eat them. When worker ants come across these seeds they carry them back to their nest. Here, the food body is eaten and the seed is tossed into the waste chamber – the perfect place for a new plant to start its life.

The bad

Despite all of these ingenious plant tactics, humans are making it trickier for new plants to grow.

Covering the ground with concrete and tarmac prevents seeds from reaching the soil.

Fewer animals left in the wild means fewer animals are available to transport seeds.

The good

You can make good choices that help seeds do their job.

Don't use weed killer on your plants, as it will stop new plants growing.

Try to avoid covering over the green space around you.

29

Biodiversity of animals

The world is full of incredible plants and animals. Every single one of them is important, because they all play a role in maintaining life on Earth.

A not-so-wild world

Sometimes we forget that all plants and animals matter, and we act in a way that causes them harm. Once upon a time, the whole world was wild. Now, after humans have explored and exploited almost every part of the planet, there are very few truly wild spaces left.

If you put them all together, the world's insects, spiders, and crustaceans would be

17 times as heavy

as the world's humans.

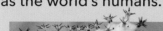

Cecropia moth caterpillar

Peacock spider

Vampire crab

Picasso bug

If we **weighed** all of the **mammals on Earth...**

...4% would be wild animals

...36% would be humans

Birds

Less than one-third of the world's birds are wild. Most of them are bred by humans for meat.

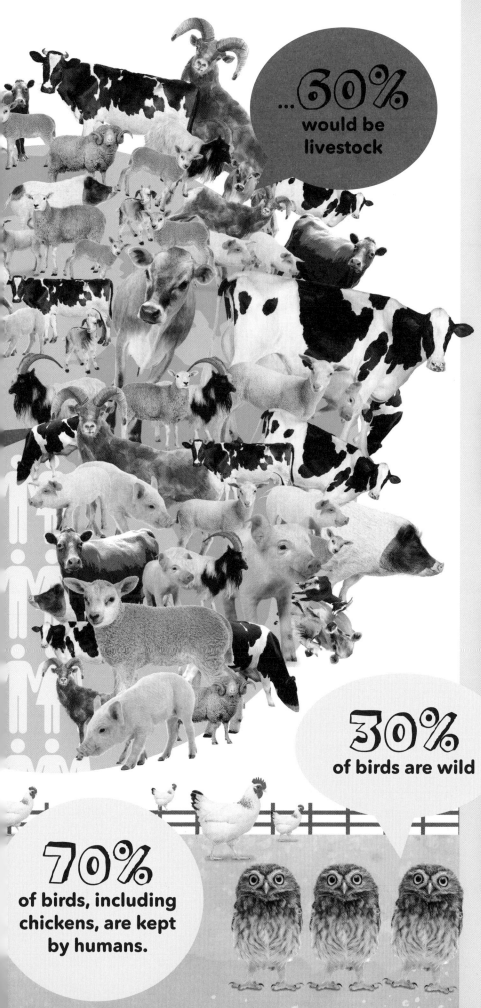

...60% would be livestock

30% of birds are wild

70% of birds, including chickens, are kept by humans.

Amazing animals

Some countries have particularly incredible animals. Madagascar, an island in Africa, is home to lots of weird and wonderful creatures:

Aye-aye

This lemur has amazing middle fingers that are extremely long. It uses them to pull grubs from the holes in trees.

Ring-tailed lemur

The fluffy striped tails of these creatures can act as a flag. Holding their tails in the air helps them to keep their group together.

Tomato frog

This bright red frog releases a toxic substance through its skin when it feels threatened.

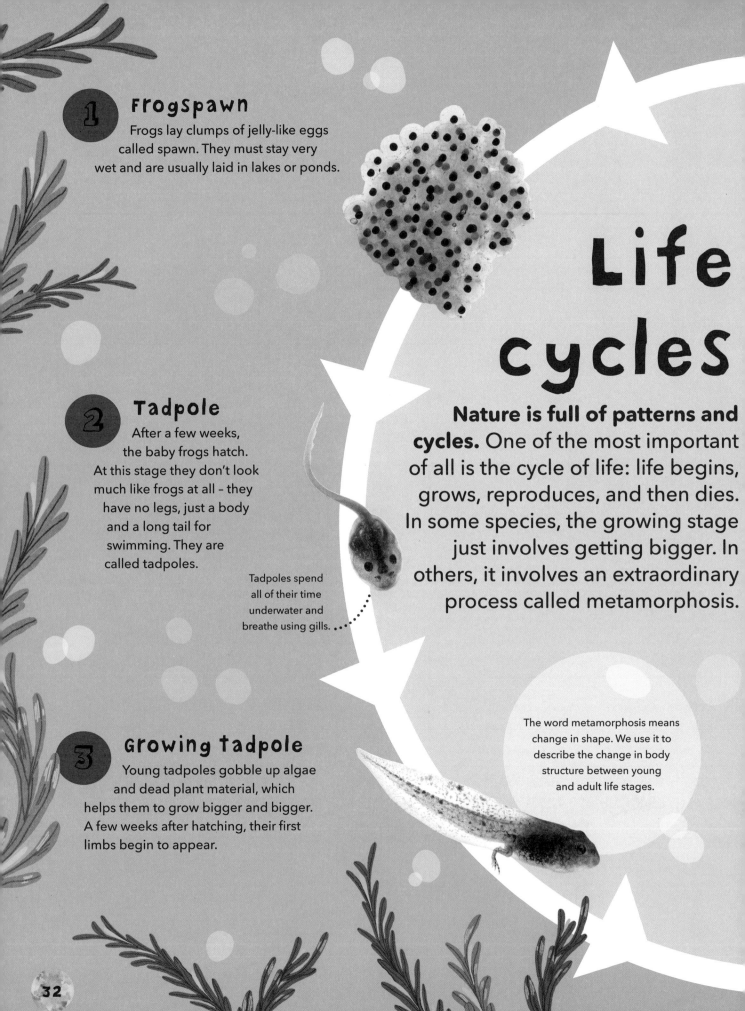

Life cycles

Nature is full of patterns and cycles. One of the most important of all is the cycle of life: life begins, grows, reproduces, and then dies. In some species, the growing stage just involves getting bigger. In others, it involves an extraordinary process called metamorphosis.

1 Frogspawn
Frogs lay clumps of jelly-like eggs called spawn. They must stay very wet and are usually laid in lakes or ponds.

2 Tadpole
After a few weeks, the baby frogs hatch. At this stage they don't look much like frogs at all – they have no legs, just a body and a long tail for swimming. They are called tadpoles.

Tadpoles spend all of their time underwater and breathe using gills.

3 Growing tadpole
Young tadpoles gobble up algae and dead plant material, which helps them to grow bigger and bigger. A few weeks after hatching, their first limbs begin to appear.

The word metamorphosis means change in shape. We use it to describe the change in body structure between young and adult life stages.

Frogs belong to a group of animals that spend their time between land and water, called amphibians. Newts, salamanders, and toads are all amphibians.

Breeding time

Frogs usually start to breed two to three years after hatching. They mate in the spring, then lay frogspawn to start the cycle once again.

Mate mission

Frogs and toads often return to the place they hatched in order to breed. Sometimes this involves crossing busy roads.

During the mating season, toad patrols, manned by volunteers, protect the migrating amphibians as they make their way back to their breeding grounds.

5

Adult frog

When the frog is fully grown, it can spend its life between both land and water. Adult frogs feed on invertebrates such as flies, slugs, and snails.

The froglet stays close to the water until it loses its tail.

4

Froglet

The tadpole develops its four legs and replaces its gills with lungs, allowing it to leave the water and venture onto dry land. This stage is known as a froglet.

Minibeasts

They may be small, but minibeasts (or invertebrates) play a mighty role in looking after our planet.

It is vital that we care for and protect them.

Providing food

Invertebrates are eaten in their thousands by birds, reptiles, amphibians, small mammals, fish, and other invertebrates.

Cleaning up

Minibeasts are not fussy eaters – in fact, they're happy to eat many of the things we find disgusting. Poo, dead animals, and plant waste are all on the menu for invertebrates.

The bad

As a result of human actions, insect numbers are plummeting across the planet. If we don't change our ways, they could be gone by 2100.

Spraying plants with pesticides kills helpful minibeasts as well as harmful ones.

Many invertebrates struggle to survive in cities, as there is limited greenery.

Many of the plants that invertebrates eat are cut down to make space for other things.

As a result of climate change, many insects are hatching too early or late.

About 30% of the world's edible crops depend on bee pollination.

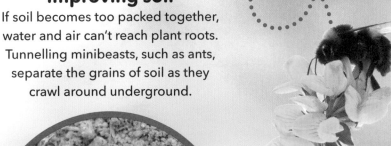

In many places, insects are considered a delicious snack. Eating insects is a great way to get protein without having a huge impact on the planet. The insects that are harvested for food are not in danger of extinction.

Improving soil

If soil becomes too packed together, water and air can't reach plant roots. Tunnelling minibeasts, such as ants, separate the grains of soil as they crawl around underground.

Pollinating

We depend on pollinating insects such as bees, wasps, moths, butterflies, and beetles to carry pollen between plants. This helps the plants and flowers we rely on for food to continue to grow.

Controlling harmful insects

Some predatory minibeasts feast on invertebrates that cause harm to humans or crops. Ladybirds are excellent at keeping aphids under control.

The good

Minibeasts reproduce very quickly, so if we make some positive changes they can still bounce back.

Make a minibeast hotel or insect haven in your outdoor space to help them thrive.

Plant insect-friendly plants that provide the energy-rich nectar insects need for food.

Make a messy corner in your garden for bugs to make a home in – don't keep it too tidy!

Never use slug pellets. They're also dangerous to dogs, birds, and hedgehogs.

Natural engineering

Beavers are nature's chainsaws, famous for their ability to cut down trees and use them to build dams across rivers. These dams help create wetlands, which provide homes for many other animals, capture carbon, reduce flooding, and store water to prevent droughts.

Engineers

Beavers are sometimes called "ecosystem engineers", because their actions greatly change the habitats they live in. Their dams are incredible structures, built from branches, trunks, mud, and plants. As well as changing the path of rivers, the dams filter water, removing pollutants, mud, and rocks.

Dam building

Beavers build dams across a fast-flowing river, forcing the water to flow more slowly.

A beaver's bright orange teeth are made strong with iron.

A beaver's wide, flat tail and webbed feet help to steer it through the water.

Bring back beavers

Beavers have disappeared from many places, but reintroduction programmes are changing that. In Scotland, beavers were brought back in 2009 after being hunted to extinction there more than 400 years ago.

Beavers and humans

Beavers were once hunted for their fur and meat. More recently they have suffered from pollution and habitat loss. Luckily, people are beginning to realize how important beavers are and are treating them with more respect.

Beavers are excellent swimmers – they can stay underwater for up to 15 minutes.

The slower flow of the water means that stones and sand get laid on the river bed, making it higher.

The river gets deeper and wider. In the slower water, beavers can build larger, more stable dams.

Behind the dams, water spills out onto the area around it and a wetland habitat is created.

Urban animals

More and more animals are making their homes in our cities. This can be because they've been driven out of their natural habitats, or because they're attracted by the food, shelter, and warmth on offer.

Living in our houses

Whether your home is in a big city or a quiet suburb, there are sure to be animals, such as the ones below, sheltering somewhere inside.

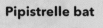
Pipistrelle bat

Tokay gecko

Funnel web spider

Ladybird

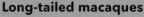
Swifts
Swifts make nests under roof eaves.

Long-tailed macaques
Many of the animals that live in cities are secretive and timid, but not long-tailed macaques. These cheeky monkeys will pinch food straight from people's hands.

Butterflies

Herring gull

Raccoon

Raccoons will eat almost anything. They dig through bins in search of tasty scraps.

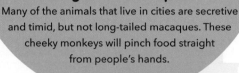
Spotted hyena

Black bear

Coati

Cockroach

Scavengers
Some animals will happily eat our leftover food. Animals that feed on the food that we throw away are known as scavengers.

Night-time

While you are tucked up
in your bed at night,
cities bustle with activity.

Leopard

**Nankeen
night
heron**

**Amur
hedgehog**

Water dragon
Water dragons are a very
common sight in the city of
Sydney, Australia.

Reptiles

Snakes and lizards are often seen in
urban spaces. While some are attracted
to the warmth of pavements, others
hide away in sewers underground.

**Reticulated
python**

Sharing our cities

While cities will never support as much
wildlife as the habitats they have
replaced, there are plenty of ways we can
help make our cities more animal-friendly.

In Singapore, Oriental pied hornbills almost
disappeared completely as they could not find
anywhere to nest. Now there are nest boxes
for them all around the city.

Making a small hole in the bottom of your fence
allows hedgehogs to pass from garden to
garden as they search for food.

One of the best ways to attract new wildlife
to a city is to build a pond. No matter how big
or small it is, it will soon be teeming with life.

Nature's recyclers

Vulture

Crab

Dung fly

Hyena

Millipede

Tasmanian devil

Sea star

Komodo dragon

Virginia opossum

Fungus

Sea cucumber

Bacteria

In nature, nothing goes to waste. Everything produced by animals and plants is recycled by nature's clean-up crew. We rely on these amazing creatures to keep the planet neat and tidy, as well as to release valuable nutrients so that they can be used again.

Making a meal of it

Keeping the planet clean is a big task, so these members of the recycling crew each perform different roles to get the job done.

All animals poo, so if nobody took on the job of clearing it up, the planet would soon be full of it. Luckily, certain species of beetle, maggot, and fly are **poo eaters**, who break down the important nutrients in poo to be reused.

Scavengers break up items of waste, such as animal carcasses, into smaller pieces. These eaters aren't fussy – they will eat almost any meat they come across. Scavengers such as crabs are important in cleaning up the ocean.

Detritivores are responsible for gobbling up the decaying remains of dead plants and animals. Worms, millipedes, dung flies, woodlice, sea cucumbers, and banana slugs are all types of detritivores.

carrion copycats

Some plants and fungi mimic the smell of carrion (decaying flesh). The stench attracts insects, that then pollinate them.

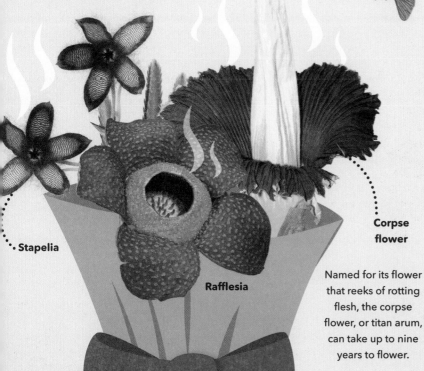

Stapelia

Rafflesia

Corpse flower

Named for its flower that reeks of rotting flesh, the corpse flower, or titan arum, can take up to nine years to flower.

The bad

Many of the materials created by humans can't be broken down by natural processes. They end up polluting the ground, water, and air.

The good

Try to use natural materials that will break down into nutrients that can be reused by plants and animals.

Migration

While some animals stay in the same place for their entire lives, others travel huge distances in search of food or a place to raise their young. This mass movement of animals from one place to another is called migration.

The Great Migration

Animals often migrate in large numbers, but none in such huge groups as the wildebeest. Every year more than one million of these extraordinary antelopes cross the African savannah on a treacherous journey between Kenya and Tanzania, as they follow the rains. They are usually accompanied by zebras and gazelles.

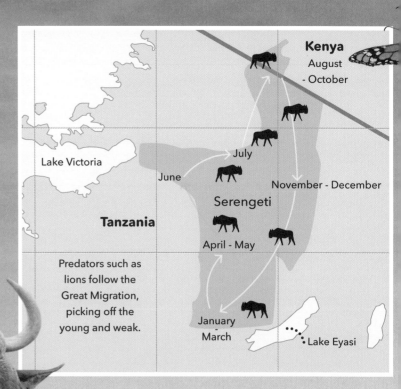

Lake Victoria

Tanzania

Kenya
August - October

July

June

November - December

Serengeti

April - May

January - March

Predators such as lions follow the Great Migration, picking off the young and weak.

Lake Eyasi

The Great Migration is the world's longest overland migration.

At the start of the migration, around half a million wildebeest calves are born. They must learn to walk straight away if they are to keep up with the herds.

christmas island red crab

Each year on Christmas Island, millions of red crabs emerge from the forest and migrate to the ocean to lay their eggs. The cast of crabs looks like a huge red carpet being rolled down the road.

Sadly, the future of monarch butterflies is threatened by changing weather conditions and habitat loss in both their summer and winter homes.

monarch butterfly

Every autumn, monarch butterflies travel 4,800 km (3,000 miles) from their summer homes in the northern USA and Canada to their winter habitats in California and Mexico. They use their in-built compass to find their way.

Evolution

The world is constantly changing, which means animals must be constantly changing too. Sometimes, human actions make these changes happen very quickly, so animals must be able to adapt quickly in order to thrive and survive.

The peppered moth's colour change is all down to a single difference in its genetic code called the cortex gene.

⚠ Peppered moth

Peppered moths are usually pale and speckled – the perfect camouflage against trees. When darker forms of the moth hatch, they are spotted by birds and eaten before they can pass on their colouring to their young. During the Industrial Revolution, trees turned black with soot, so pale moths became easy prey and dark ones grew more common.

No more pollution

Most air pollution comes from burning fossil fuels. This releases tiny particles into the air, which can be very dangerous for any animals that breathe them in, including humans. If you need to travel and don't have far to go, choose to walk or cycle instead of taking the car, so you are not adding to the air pollution problem.

In less polluted areas, the paler form of the moth is still more common.

Over time, the most helpful features become more common and the whole species gradually evolves.

Evolution

Charles Darwin was a naturalist from the 1800s. He noticed that even within the same species each individual was slightly different. He believed that some changes gave animals a greater chance of survival, so they could pass on their genes to the next generation. He called this evolution by natural selection.

Extinction

For as long as animals have been evolving, they have been going extinct too. It is a natural and normal part of life and evolution. Throughout history, there have been several periods of time when animals have gone extinct much more quickly than usual. These periods are called mass extinctions.

We are currently in the midst of the sixth mass extinction, because of the way humans are behaving.

More than **900** species have gone extinct since 1500...

... and more than **500** species of animal are on the brink of extinction right now.

Important animals

Plants, animals, and other living things rely on and interact with each other in complicated ways. Because of this, every organism has a vital role to play in supporting the other organisms around it. Protecting endangered species helps to protect all species.

Back from the brink

Humpback whale

Prized for their meat and blubber, humpback whales were heavily hunted in the 1960s and almost disappeared. But after a ban on whaling was passed in 1986, their numbers recovered and the population is now almost back at its original size.

These birds were often poisoned by the lead bullets used to kill big animals.

California condor

As a result of poisoning, habitat loss, and hunting, just 22 California condors remained in the wild in 1982. Thanks to a captive breeding programme, there are now more than 300.

conservation action has saved 40 species of mammals and birds from extinction since 1993.

Blue iguana

This huge lizard from Grand Cayman island in the Caribbean is one of the longest-living lizards, and can live for more than 60 years. By 2001 there were only around 30 left in the wild, but thanks to a conservation programme in Grand Cayman there are now more than 1,000.

Rediscovered

Hula painted frog

In 2011 a Hula painted frog was found hidden in an overgrown patch of swamp by a park ranger. It was thought to have gone extinct more than a decade earlier.

Lord Howe Island stick insect

These huge stick insects were thought to have gone extinct in 1918 after black rats were introduced to their island, but a small population was discovered in 2001.

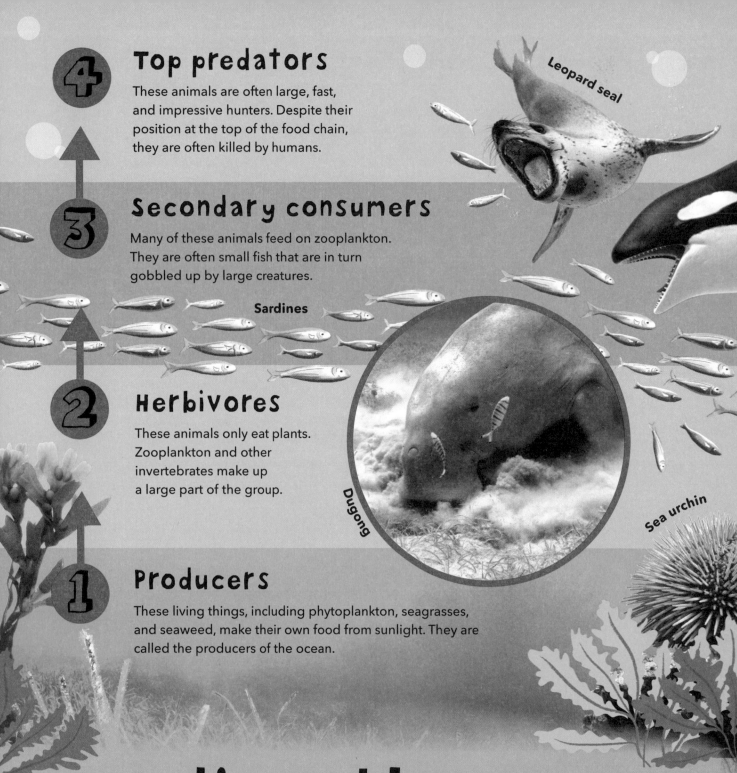

4 Top predators

These animals are often large, fast, and impressive hunters. Despite their position at the top of the food chain, they are often killed by humans.

Leopard seal

3 Secondary consumers

Many of these animals feed on zooplankton. They are often small fish that are in turn gobbled up by large creatures.

Sardines

2 Herbivores

These animals only eat plants. Zooplankton and other invertebrates make up a large part of the group.

Dugong

Sea urchin

1 Producers

These living things, including phytoplankton, seagrasses, and seaweed, make their own food from sunlight. They are called the producers of the ocean.

Feeding the ocean

The oceans are teeming with life. We know of more than 230,000 marine species – that's a lot of hungry mouths to feed. Ocean food chains are often interconnected, meaning that each and every plant and animal plays a part in feeding the rest.

Orca

Blue whales are the biggest animals ever to have lived. In spite of their enormous size, their diet is mostly made up of tiny shrimp-like crustaceans called krill. A blue whale can eat as much as four tonnes of krill every day – about the same weight as six cows!

Sea turtle

Zooplankton

Plankton

Any small organism that drifts along with the current is called plankton. Phytoplankton is the name given to the plants in this group of organisms. The animals are called zooplankton, and include krill and the babies of bigger animals such as fish and crustaceans.

⚠ The bad

Human pollution often ends up in the food chain. Plankton usually eat these toxic chemicals first, and they travel right up to the top predators.

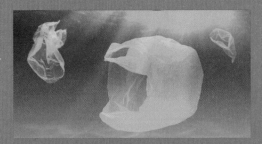

We have poured so much plastic into the ocean that it can now be found in every layer – even in the very deepest trenches.

By taking too many of the largest, healthiest fish from the ocean to eat, humans have made it almost impossible for some species to breed. This leaves little for the top predators to eat.

The good

By cutting down on the amount of plastic you buy and throw away, you will reduce the amount that reaches the oceans.

If you eat fish, choose a species that is sustainably managed and has been caught responsibly.

coral reefs

Known as the rainforests of the sea, coral reefs are bursting with marine life. Although they occupy less than 0.1 per cent of the ocean, they provide shelter and protection for 25 per cent of all ocean species.

Why do we need them?

As well as housing thousands of species, coral reefs anchor and stabilize the seabed, and protect sea shores from powerful waves. By absorbing and spreading out the waves' energy, corals act as crucial buffers between open ocean and land.

Parrotfish

...700 species of coral...

coral reefs are home to over 4,000 species of fish...

...and thousands of other species of plants and animals.

Scientists estimate that in total more than one million species of plants and animals are associated with the coral reef ecosystem.

The challenges they face

Corals and algae rely on each other to survive. When exposed to too much heat, pollution, air, or sunlight, corals become stressed and the colourful algae within them leave. As a result, corals are left bleached and vulnerable. Half of the world's coral reefs have already been severely damaged. Losing all of our coral reefs could mean losing a quarter of all ocean species.

It takes a long time for corals to recover after being bleached, as they only grow around 2 cm (1 in) a year.

Rainforests

Home to more than three million different species, rainforests are the most biodiverse ecosystems on Earth. While many animals rely on rainforests for food and shelter, rainforests rely on the animals that live inside them.

Fire!

During hot weather, small forest fires are not unusual. However, our changing climate and deforestation is making them more common and ferocious – bad news for forest plants and animals.

About six per cent of land on Earth is covered by tropical rainforests. They are home to more than half our land animals and plants.

Peccary

Pig-like peccaries love nothing better than wallowing in cool, refreshing mud. They make pits in the earth that fill with rainwater and stay wet all year round, attracting fish, frogs, dragonflies, and snakes.

African forest elephant

By stomping on young plants and ripping up small bushes and trees, African forest elephants thin out the undergrowth. This allows big trees to grow larger than ever, so they can absorb vast amounts of carbon from the atmosphere.

The bad

Rainforests and the plants and animals that live in them face many serious threats.

Poachers kill some animals to sell their body parts or steal their young.

Trees are being cut down at an alarming rate for their wood.

Forests are destroyed so we can mine for valuable resources beneath them.

As more people live in or visit forests, animals face risks such as being hit by cars or hunted.

Lyrebird

Lyrebirds forage for food by scratching through dirt on the forest floor. This mixes up the top layers of the soil, allowing burrowing invertebrates and important nutrients to travel deeper into the soil.

Buttress roots

In tropical rainforests, the highest amounts of nutrients are usually found in the shallow top layers of soil. Rainforest trees often have enormous roots called buttress roots above the ground, where they can access these nutrients.

Southern cassowary

Cassowaries love to gobble up forest fruits. After digesting the fruit, the birds poo out the seeds, which then sprout into new plants. They have been known to carry the seeds of more than 200 different types of plant.

Leaf-cutter ant

Despite being so small, leaf-cutter ants can have a big effect on their environment. By removing leaves from the tree canopy, they allow more light to hit the ground, increasing its temperature and encouraging new plants to grow.

The good

Thinking before you buy certain things is the best way to protect forests. The most helpful thing you can do is to simply buy less!

If you need to buy something new, think about where it came from and what impact it has had on the world.

If you buy a product made from trees, such as furniture or paper, look out for the FSC logo.

Whenever you can, try to buy things second-hand instead of brand new.

Choose recycled cardboard, tissue, and paper.

Mountains

Mountains can be found all over our planet – even at the bottom of the ocean! Conditions at great heights can be extremely harsh, so the plants and animals that live in alpine habitats are highly adapted to life on the slopes.

> The adaptations that allow mountain species to survive cold, harsh climates make them vulnerable to increasing temperatures.

Snow leopard
These big cats were hunted almost to extinction by humans, and are now threatened by loss of prey and habitat. They are extremely shy and well-camouflaged, making them tricky to spot in the wild.

Viscacha
Despite looking like rabbits, mountain viscachas are more closely related to chinchillas. They use their large hind legs to jump from rock to rock, and keep themselves warm with a thick layer of fluffy fur.

The bad
While climate change contributes to mountain species losing their habitats and prey, a lot of mountain wildlife is threatened by human visitors to the mountains, too.

The average climber attempting to summit Mount Everest produces 8 kg (17.5 lb) of rubbish.

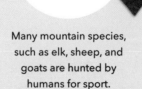

Many mountain species, such as elk, sheep, and goats are hunted by humans for sport.

If their habitat was destroyed, alpine animals would struggle to survive elsewhere.

Alpine bumblebee

Alpine bumblebees can be found hovering at heights of over 5,000 m (16,400 ft). While they are able to fly even higher than this, they can only travel as high as the plants they feed on grow, or they will run out of energy.

Kea

Kea are rare alpine parrots found in the mountains of New Zealand. They are cheeky birds that are fascinated by humans – they've even been found rummaging through tourists' bags in search of treasure!

Nilgiri tahr

The nimble Nilgiri tahr expertly climbs across rocky slopes in southern India. It came close to extinction in the 20th century, with less than 100 remaining, but thanks to conservation, its numbers are now on the rise.

Mountain gorilla

Living in war-torn areas, mountain gorillas have suffered greatly thanks to humans. But there's good news: they are now the one great ape whose population is increasing.

The good

People are working hard to reduce human impact on mountain habitats, as well as coming up with clever ways to support the animals that live there.

Wild corridors between protected mountain habitats allow threatened mountain species to move around safely.

Climbers of Mount Everest are rewarded if they return with more than 8kg (17.5 lb) of waste.

Working together with the people who live in the mountains is the best way to protect these valuable habitats.

Deserts

Deserts are places of extremes.
They are often extremely hot and dry with poor quality soils, making it hard for plants to grow. The animals that live in this harsh habitat must be well adapted in order to survive.

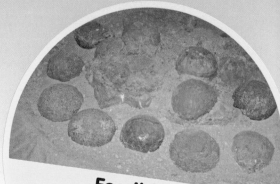

Fossil finds
Many amazing fossils have been found in the desert, including fossilized forests, dinosaur bones, and even dinosaur nests!

Sand dunes are masses of loose sand
that crawl across the desert, blown by strong and steady winds.

Shield shrimp
It doesn't often rain in the desert, so when desert pools are filled, these freshwater shrimps must hatch and mature quickly in order to complete their lifecycle before the water dries up again.

Sandfish
These desert lizards are sand specialists. They spend almost their entire lives buried in the sand, using vibrations to hunt their prey. Their bodies are perfectly adapted to slither through the grains as if they are swimming.

The bad
Around the world, as soil quality declines, areas that were once forest are rapidly turning to desert. This is called desertification. While deserts are incredible ecosystems, animal populations suited to forest habitats cannot survive in these tougher conditions.

Erosion increases when trees are cut down, as their roots no longer stabilize the soil.

When too much vegetation is eaten by livestock, soil is more easily washed away.

As global temperatures increase, many places are becoming drier and drier.

Kangaroo rat

Clever kangaroo rats can survive in the desert without ever drinking any water – they get all the moisture they need from their food. To save water, they produce concentrated wee and lose very little water through their skin.

Gopher tortoise

These tortoises dig deep burrows under the sand to escape the Sun's heat. But they are not the only ones that use them – more than 100 different species have been known to shelter inside desert tortoise burrows.

Saguaro cactus

Not much can survive the tough conditions of the Sonoran Desert of Mexico and the USA, but the Saguaro cactus thrives. Its fruits and seeds feed many birds and its flesh is carved out by woodpeckers to build their nests.

Scorpion

Many scorpions can be found in deserts. They usually hide in cool burrows during the hottest part of the day and emerge to hunt at night. Their tough exoskeletons protect them from the Sun's rays and stop water loss.

The good

Many of the changes we can make to prevent desertification are to do with changing the way we raise animals and grow crops. Do some research and try to buy your food from farms that are growing their crops responsibly.

Grow plants, as their roots will hold the soil in place and prevent it from being blown or washed away.

Graze fewer animals in each field and keep changing fields so the ground can recover.

Use earth dams, drip irrigation, and magic stones to reduce water waste.

Wetlands

Like enormous sponges, wetlands soak up heavy rainfalls, preventing floods and attracting all sorts of incredible animals. With so much water stored away, wonderful wetlands stay wet even during dry periods, providing water and food for wildlife when times are tough.

carbon keepers

Wetlands are incredible at storing carbon: they are estimated to hold more than a third of the world's land-based carbon stores. When wetlands are disturbed, they release large amounts of greenhouse gases into the atmosphere, so protecting them will help to prevent further climate change.

Bogland areas are often destroyed to remove peat for use in compost and and as a fuel.

> Peatlands store twice as much carbon as all the world's forests combined.

Marshes, swamps, bogs, fens, rivers, floodplains, reedbeds, lakes, deltas,

Gator holes

In the Everglades National Park, USA, American alligators dig out small ponds with their feet and snouts to help them stay cool. Many other animals benefit from these ponds including fish, snakes, turtles, insects, and birds.

An in-built snorkel allows the snail to breathe fresh air from above the water when oxygen in the water is low.

Apple snail

When microbes break down plant waste in the Pantanal region of South America, the water's oxygen levels drop dramatically. The apple snail gobbles up the decaying plants so that oxygen increases and other animals may return.

The bad

Despite being so important, 87 per cent of the world's wetlands have been lost over the last 300 years.

We have drained thousands of acres of wetlands to provide land for building.

80 per cent of the world's wastewater is released into wetlands untreated.

When foreign species, such as this signal crayfish, are introduced into wetlands they can be very damaging for native species.

estuaries, mudflats, mangroves, and coral reefs are all types of wetland.

Hidden underground

There are all sorts of wonderful things hidden deep underground, including metals, minerals, and fossils. For hundreds of years, humans have dug into the ground in search of treasure, and along the way we have made some extraordinary discoveries.

Fossils

Fossils give us clues about what Earth was like a long time ago. They are sometimes discovered by accident, but in some places fossils are so common that people travel there especially to hunt for them.

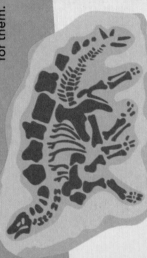

Coal

Fossil fuels

Oil, coal, and gas are all fossil fuels – natural materials that are burned to generate power. Burning fossil fuels is bad for the environment and our fossil fuel reserves won't last forever, so it is vital that we use more renewable sources of energy, such as wind and solar, instead.

Peat

Peat is formed from the breakdown of dead plants in bogs and peatlands. It is important to the planet because it stores vast quantities of carbon. Peat is mined to burn and to use in gardens as fertilizer. This releases the carbon that it stores and destroys bogland habitats, which are home to many rare animals and plants.

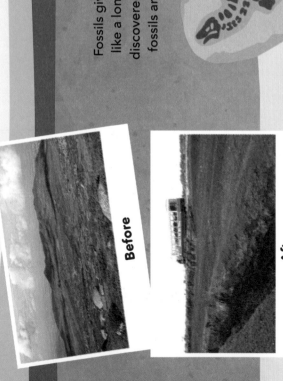

Before

After

Mines

The soil and rock beneath our feet is made up of lots of different materials. There are more of certain materials in certain places. When humans discover an area that is rich in a material they consider to be valuable, they often set up mines to extract it. This is very damaging to the plants and animals that live in the area.

Dangerous work

Sometimes the people that work in mines are made ill through contact with the materials they are mining.

Poisoning the water

Mining sometimes produces toxic waste, which can pollute the local waterways. This is dangerous for the animals and people that rely on them for drinking water.

Electronics

Many of the materials we mine are used to make electronics. Sadly, instead of repairing old electronics when they break, people often just buy new ones. This means that a lot of mined materials go to waste.

Mines are very deep, often extending many kilometres below the surface. Building them is a tricky task that requires lots of specialized machinery.

Mined minerals

Copper

Large copper mines can be found in Chile and Indonesia. Copper is used in wires, pipes, and machinery.

Aluminium

Even though aluminium can be easily recycled, a lot still goes to landfill. In fact, landfill sites are so full of metals that people are considering mining in them.

Gold, silver, and diamonds

These materials are all mined because of how they look. They're often used to make jewellery and expensive goods.

What can we do?

Repair electronics when they break. Don't throw away an item that still works just because you want a new one.

Use renewable energy sources, such as solar panels, instead of fossil fuels.

Choose peat-free compost for your garden and plants.

Sea ice

Each winter, large volumes of seawater in the polar oceans freeze to form sea ice. Most of this ice melts again in the summer, but some remains all year round. Many animals depend on sea ice for survival and it also plays a role in keeping our planet cool.

Polar bear

Large, stable areas of sea ice are crucial to polar bears' survival. They travel long distances on it or use it to rest and build dens. If sea ice shrinks, polar bears will find it harder to hunt and may not have enough energy to breed or feed their cubs. If we lose sea ice, we are likely to lose polar bears too.

Protective layer

Sea ice forms a layer on the edge of ice shelves (floating extensions of land ice). This layer protects the ice shelves from wind and waves, and keeps the water below it warm.

Seal

Several seal species, including the harp seal, spotted seal, and ringed seal, rarely come to land, so they are heavily dependent on sea ice. Their babies are born on the ice, where they are left while their mothers hunt below the surface. These animals would have a hard time adapting to ice-free summers.

Narwhals

Without the protection of sea ice, narwhals would be much more vulnerable to hunting by orcas and people.

Light reflector

The white colour of ice reflects much more light and heat than the dark surface of the surrounding water. This helps to keep the planet cool.

Walrus

Walruses feed on clams from the sea floor, using the sea ice as a diving platform. They also travel across the ice in search of new feeding grounds. If the sea ice melts, walruses will have to find new ways to feed in order to survive.

Myth busted

Just as drinks containing ice cubes don't overflow when the ice cubes melt, sea levels don't increase when sea ice melts.

We can save sea ice by combatting climate change.

Ice algae

The algae that grows on the bottom of sea ice is a crucial food source for many of the animals that live above and below the ice. As it forms the base of the food chain in this ecosystem, many predators also depend on ice algae for their survival too.

The bad

Thanks to climate change, sea ice has been melting since the 1970s. Soon it will disappear entirely, at least for part of the year.

Ice-free summers would be a disaster for the animals that depend on ice sheets.

The good

Try making these simple changes to reduce your contribution to global warming.

Switch off electrical appliances when you leave a room to reduce your electricity usage.

Walk or use public transport instead of taking the car to reduce greenhouse gas emissions.

Ask your grown-ups to consider switching to renewable sources of electricity.

You can create your own wild anywhere!

Stachys lanata

Bees and other nectar-feeding insects can't travel far without stopping for a sugary snack. Nectar-rich flowers provide them with a pick-me-up to help them on their way.

Marigold

Put water in a saucer for thirsty animals to drink from.

Add sticks so that smaller creatures can climb in and out.

Bacopa snowflake

Any space is good space

You don't need much space to create a wild patch. Animals will love anywhere you provide, whether it's a balcony, windowsill, or corner of the garden.

Use an old welly as a planter

Verbena

Clover

Wild pansy

Choose peat-free compost.

Turn an old, broken cup into a plant pot.

Protect your patch

It's not difficult to create a wild haven for the creatures living around you. It just takes a little time and thought into what they will like best.

Plant wild flowers
Choose a mixture of wild flowers that bloom throughout the year so that hungry pollinators will always have nectar to feed on.

Let the ivy grow
Ivy provides a safe hiding place for birds and other wildlife. Its flowers and seeds are also good sources of food and pollen.

Hedgehog hideaways
Leave a pile of leaves, sticks, or logs in your garden. It will make the perfect place for hedgehogs to nest, hibernate, and forage for bugs.

Nature's daily miracles

Our world is a busy and hectic place, so it can sometimes be hard to switch off. One of the best ways to relax is to spend some time in nature. Step outside, take a deep breath, and admire the world around you. Try these tricks to help you connect with nature.

Spending time in nature makes us calmer, healthier, and more positive.

Watch the Sun rise

As the Sun peeks over the horizon, feel its rays begin to warm your skin and give you energy for a new day.

Watch the Sun set

Find a quiet spot to see the Sun go down. Admire the colours it paints across the sky. Try to clear your head of worries.

See the stars appear

Look up at the night sky as the stars begin to appear. How many other people do you think are gazing up at the same stars?

connect with your environment

Go for a swim

Walk barefoot

Sit under a tree

Hear the birds sing

Birdsong has been proven to make people feel happier and less stressed. Listen out for joyful bird tunes, especially on calm spring days.

Weather watch

What pictures can you spot in the clouds? From rainbows to snowflakes, nature is full of beautiful things to keep you entertained.

Glossary

agriculture
Growing crops and raising animals for food

aurora
Natural displays of colourful light in the night sky that happen at the north and south poles of some planets

biodiversity
The variety of plants and animals that live in an area

carcass
The dead body of an animal

conservation
Protecting environments and plant and animal life

dam
A barrier that holds back water

decomposer
A living thing that breaks down dead matter to create nutrients

deforestation
Cutting down trees and destroying forests

ecosystem
A community of living things and their non-living environment – including the soil, water, and air around them

erosion
Gradual wearing away of rocks due to water and weather

evolution
Process where a species changes, over many generations, to suit its environment

fertilize
Spread a natural or chemical substance on land or plants, in order to make the plants grow well

fossil fuel
A fuel made from animals and plants that died millions of years ago, such as coal, oil, and natural gas

fruiting body
The part of a fungus in which the spores are produced

galaxy
Huge group of stars, gas, and dust held together by gravity

genetic code
The arrangement of chemicals within genes

germinate
When a seed starts to grow

gravity
Invisible force that pulls objects towards each other

greenhouse gas
Gases in the Earth's atmosphere that trap heat and warm the planet

invertebrate
Animal that does not have a backbone

landfill
Place where rubbish is buried in the ground

livestock
Farm animals such as cows and sheep

metamorphosis
Process by which some animals transform themselves into a different form from youth to adulthood

microbe
Microscopic organism

migrate
Move from one country or region to go and live in another

naturalist
Person who studies nature

natural selection
Process in which the best adapted living things are able to survive and pass on their good characteristics when they reproduce

orbit
The path an object takes around another due to gravity, such as how planets travel around the Sun

organism
Living thing

ozone layer
Area in the Earth's atmosphere that protects the surface from the Sun's harmful rays

poacher
Person who hunts or catches animals or fish illegally

poultry
Birds kept by humans for their eggs, meat, or feathers

predator
Animal that hunts other living animals for food

regenerate
When a living thing regrows after being damaged

renewable
Type of energy that will not run out, such as solar power

Single-celled organism
Very simple living thing that consists of one cell

sustainable
Energy or materials that can keep going for a long time

Index

Acknowledgements

DK would like to thank the following:

Rituraj Singh for picture research, and Susie Rae for indexing.

The publisher would like to thank the following for their kind permission to reproduce their photographs:

(Key: a-above; b-below/bottom; c-centre; f-far; l-left; r-right; t-top)

123RF.com: alekss 38clb, anthonycz 12c, 44bl, aopsan / Natthawut Panyosaeng 41crb, Tim Hester 40c (centipede), Eric Isselee 18crb, Andrea Izzotti 53cl, Kittipong Jirasukhanont 9tl, jukurae 11tr, Piotr Krzeslak 65crb, madllen 25c, mhgallery 42bl, Dmytro Nikitin 52bc (truck), onairjiw / Sataporn Jiwjalaen 7crb, Ekaterina Pereverzeva 67cb, Peterz / Peter Zaharov 39bc, Isselee Eric Philippe 43cla, sonsedskaya / Yuliia Sonsedska 38crb, Thuansak Srilao 56br, swavo 49c, Thawat Tanhai 16-17 (butterfly x2), weenvector 16-17 (reed x4), Richard Whitcombe 11cra, PAN XUNBIN 40cl, zhudifeng 29tr; **Alamy Stock Photo:** Ashley Cooper pics 21tl, BIOSPHOTO / Adam Fletcher 30cb, blickwinkel / F. Hecker 55tl, blickwinkel / H. Bellmann / F. Hecker 23bl, Blue Planet Archive EDA 18-19 (background), Rick & Nora Bowers 27tl, Neil Bowman 39ca, David Tipling Photo Library 56tr, Chad Ehlers 8-9ca, Richard Ellis 59tl, Enlightened Images / Gary Crabbe 56cl, Barry Freeman 57tl, Tim Gainey 26c, Helmut Göthel Symbiosis 30bl, imageBROKER / Michaela Walch 37tr, Ivan Kuzmin 57cr, Emmanuel Lattes 23cla, Frans Lemmens 56cr, Buddy Mays 23cra, Minden Pictures / Sean Crane 27clb, Minden Pictures / Stephen Belcher 43t, William Mullins 57tr, Nature Photographers Ltd / Paul R. Sterry 49cb, Nature Picture Library / Jurgen Freund 28clb, Nature Picture Library / MYN / Tim Hunt 33ca, 33clb, Nature Picture Library / Will Burrard-Lucas 47clb, Brian Overcast 43cb, Roger Phillips 20cl, David Plummer 23crb, Lee Rentz 19c, REUTERS / NIR ELIAS 47crb, SuperStock / RGB Ventures / Rainbow / Skip Moody 30clb, Nick Upton 36bl; **Corbis:** Ocean 10bc (toilet); **Dorling Kindersley:** Jerry Young and Jerry Young 34 (pill woodlouse x2), 64bl, Cotswold Farm Park, Gloucestershire 30-31 (bagot goat x4), Dan Crisp 8-9 (meteor x4), Aleesha Nandhra 1 (beaver), 1 (bee), 2 (ladybird), 2 (spider), 2br, 3 (bee), 3 (roly poly), 6cra, 12-13c, 14 (bee), 19 (orange fishes), 20 (millipede), 20-21 (ants), 23cb, 24br, 25cl, 26 (sphinx moth x2), 29tl (Ceratocaryum argenteum seed), 29cl, 32-33 (seaweed and bubbles), 34 (bee), 35clb, 36-37 (beaver illustrations x 5), 41c, 58tr, 64 (ladybird), 64 (roly poly), 64 (spider), 65 (bee), 70-71 (seaweed and bubbles), 72 (beaver x4), 72 (bee x2), Natural History Museum, London 44cra, 45cra, 48crb, RHS Hampton Court Flower Show 2014 35bc (garden); **Dreamstime.com:** 3dsculptor / Konstantin Shaklein 9tc, Aksitaykut 53bc, Aopsan / Natthawut Punyosaeng 67tl, Natalia Bachkova 34cl, Nilanjan Bhattacharya 30fcr, Buriy 15cra, Ziga Camernik 34clb, Puntasit Choksawatdikorn 49c (zooplankton), Christineg 56-57 (background), Comzeal 34bc, Conchasdiver 18cb (sponge), California Condor 47tr, Neal Cooper 29tl, Costasz 13crb, Natalya Danko 61bc, Denboma 29cra, Djahan / Vladimir Ovchinnikov 61cr, Dlehman97 / Drew Lehman 65cr, Duki84 23cb (tractor), Dule964 2tl, 25r (oak leaves x4), Dutchscenery 11cr, Ecelop 61cl, Roman Egorov 8-9b (background), Ewanchesser / Callan Chesser 40clb, Iakov Filimonov 54br, Svetlana Foote 30cr, Freezingpictures / Jan Martin Will 63cra, Galinasavina 31crb, Gallinagomedia 38cl, Galuniki 6-72 (globe on page no.s), Stefan Hermans 13tr, Eric Isselee 31 (rove goat x3), 40crb, Isselee 30-31 (arles merino sheep x4), 30-31 (gottingen minipig x4), 30-31 (sheep x3), 31 (holstein cow x4), 31 (lamb x5), 32c, 32cb, 40ca, 40crb (komodo dragon), 58tr (dragonfly), 64tr, Iulianna Est 14crb, Izanbar

48c, Jackf / Iakov Filimonov 62cla, 69crb, Javarman 31cra, Jezper 9br, Jgade 33tl, 58br, Aleksandar Jocic 17cb, Jpsdk / Jens Stolt 38-39 (butterflies), 42-43 (monarch butterflies), Jan Kamenář 52cl, Elena Kazanskaya 40c, Kirati Kicharearn 8br, Kkaplin / Kira Kaplinski 41clb, Konart 47tl, Irina Kozhemyakina 40clb (opossum), Christopher Meder 46 (background), Mille19 39cr, Duncan Noakes 41cla, Nostone 41cb, Pop Nukoonrat 67br, Okea 10bc, Sean Pavone 39crb, Petejw / Peter Wilson 52tr, Photka 49crb (bin), Photoeuphoria 49crb, Photographyfirm 41cra, Photomall 15cr, Photopips 53br, Pnwnature 35bc, Pawel Przybyszewski 41ca, Pxhidalgo / Pablo Hidalgo 23bc, 53cr, Richcareyzim / Richard Carey 48-49b (background), Rolmat / Rui Matos 8cb, Romrodinka 58-59 (background), Saaaaa 53tr, Darryn Schneider 62-63t (background), 68-69cb (background), Andrei Shupilo 34-35 (ants x6), Joe Sohm 54-55 (background), Bidouze St¥Ë_phane 52-53 (background), Stockr 17c, Subbotina 17crb (chickenn), Supertrooper 31 (dairy cow x3), Syaber / Vladyslav Siaber 15br, Jordan Tan 9cra, Trinijacobs 55cl, Sergey Uryadnikov 15tl, Usensam2007 / Roman Samokhin 30fcra, Vasiliy Vishnevskiy 67bl, Aleksandr Vorobev 34bc (buenos aires), Vvoevale 67tr, Imogen Warren 53tl, Dennis Van De Water 31br, Jolanta Wojcicka 18cb, Yocamon 52br, Zakalinka 65cra, Zanskar / Vladimir Melnik 63cla, Abeselom Zerit 54cl, Zniehf 58clb, Rudmer Zwerver 38cl (bat); **Fotolia:** apttone 61br, Eric Isselee 31bc, Olena Pantiukh 30-31cb (hen x7); **Getty Images:** EyeEm / Haryadi Bakri 27br, Moment Open / Chris Minihane 30bc, Thomas Roche 57cl; **Getty Images / iStock:** alisontoonphotographer 27cr, Robin Bouwmeester 22-23 (background), neil bowman 38ca, Rainer von Brandis 51cr, BrianAJackson 4-5 (background), 28-29 (background), 57bc, Marc Bruxelle 45tl, Roberto Campello 12clb, castigatio 20-21 (background), charliebishop 11br, cmturkmen 59cr, Gerald Corsi 55tr, danleap 30-31cb, deimagine 17tr, Iryna Dobytchina 35tc, E+ / hadynyah 55bc (woman), E+ / PeteWill 11ca, E+ / PictureLake 57br, E+ / ugurhan 16cl, E+ / ultramarinfoto 50b, eco2drew 49tc, Leonid Eremeychuk 16cb, estivillml 54cr, gene1988 14cb, GlobalP 39cla, Henrik_L 44c, 45c, Ian_Redding 29clb, 34cr, lechatnoir 53bc (girl), Lucilleb 55bc, MikeLane45 59crb, Muenz 34-35 (background), paule858 35cl, 35clb (ant nest), phototrip 39cra, Picsfive 54bc, piyaset 59cra, redmal 2-3c (background), 24-25c (background), ricardoreitmeyer 26-27 (background), RTimages 63crb, spawns 61cra, 63br, t_kimura 2-3cb (background), 24-25c (background), TShum 16-17 (background), Utopia_88 28crb, Wim Verhagen 14clb, vlad61 51b, WLDavies 42-43 (background), yotrak 56bc, zampe238 55cr, zanskar 14-15, zlikovec 14cb (pine), Zocha_K 31cr; **NASA:** NASA Earth Observatory images by Joshua Stevens, using Landsat data from the U.S. Geological Survey 19cra; **Science Photo Library:** Louise Murray 63clb; **Shutterstock.com:** Cathy Withers-Clarke 52cr, PomInPerth 39c, Westend61 on Offset / Kiko Jimenez 50cra, Danny Ye 47br

Cover images: *Front:* **Dorling Kindersley:** Aleesha Nandhra b/ (bee, earthworm & centipede); **Dreamstime.com:** Jpsdk / Jens Stolt (butterflies)

All other images © Dorling Kindersley